T0090693

Here's What I Know

I Know

Change your life through intentional focus

By

A Student of Satori

BALBOA.PRESS

A DIVISION OF HAY HOUSE

Balboa Press books may be ordered through booksellers or by contacting:

Balboa Press
A Division of Hay House
1663 Liberty Drive
Bloomington, IN 47403
www.balboapress.com
844-682-1282

Because of the dynamic nature of the Internet, any web addresses or
links contained in this book may have changed since publication and
may no longer be valid. The views expressed in this work are solely those
of the author and do not necessarily reflect the views of the publisher,
and the publisher hereby disclaims any responsibility for them.

The author of this book does not dispense medical advice or prescribe the use
of any technique as a form of treatment for physical, emotional, or medical
problems without the advice of a physician, either directly or indirectly. The
intent of the author is only to offer information of a general nature to help
you in your quest for emotional and spiritual well-being. In the event you use
any of the information in this book for yourself, which is your constitutional
right, the author and the publisher assume no responsibility for your actions.

Any people depicted in stock imagery provided by Getty Images are
models, and such images are being used for illustrative purposes only.
Certain stock imagery © Getty Images.

Print information available on the last page.

ISBN: 979-8-7652-4759-4 (sc)
ISBN: 979-8-7652-4758-7 (e)

Library of Congress Control Number: 2023922279

Balboa Press rev. date: 11/30/2023

Contents

Introduction

The beginning of my personal Satori

Write It Down

I received my first diary at about 7 years old. I enjoyed writing down my daily life events; it made me feel as though someone was listening to my every concern, disappointment, triumph, and question. Now, in my 50s, I've come to understand it wasn't just a "feeling." Someone was listening: it was me. I believe we all possess a non-physical self-that's older and wiser than our physical one. It is always loving, never judging, and attentively listens to our every desire through our feelings and focus. I've always felt its presence, but only recently have I truly understood it. My life has had its challenges, and I've experienced much self-doubt, self-pity, worry, and often, loneliness.

As I have gotten older, I frequently pick up a new journal and start new entries, reflecting on the current period of my life. Over the years, those diaries have been placed in boxes as I moved, got married, had kids, and journeyed through life. I now understand that my experiences, triumphs, and even the perceived failures are very relatable to many others—and that's what this book is about. Looking back at my childhood, young adulthood, motherhood, and now as I approach my "later" years, I recognize that much of what I believed was best came from many misguided understandings. These didn't offer tools for intentional focus on my genuine desires or the outcomes I hoped for.

I've realized that those feelings of self-doubt, self-pity, worry, and yes, loneliness, were self-inflicted, shaped by my focus at the time. Sharing these experiences, and writing about what I've learned that led me to a new understanding of my own power and the ability to influence my reality, is the story I want to tell.

My heart was in the right place, and I always came from a place of love. However, what I've now come to understand is that this doesn't mean I had no responsibility for my own life and how I affected others on their journey. I didn't realize how to intentionally manifest what I wanted, and I certainly didn't recognize that I WAS, in fact, manifesting. Growing up, I was never shown how by ANY example. I am grateful that through the years I have been blessed to be shown by some amazing people how I AM powerful and my thoughts DO become things and how to now begin to see I have control over what I get and also, what desires I still may not have in my life.

I know now that it is not my job to dictate or control another but to allow and teach only by example. If I can't live my truth and teach by example then I certainly have no place or right dictating what anyone else should do, be, desire, or believe. During the years of re-learning and realizing my knowing, the knowing I came into this journey with, that continues to remind me of my own power and ability to manifest my own desired reality by practicing my commitments to myself of focus and intention, I am guided in manifesting miracles in my life. This commitment is a continuous purposeful act that requires self-examination into how I handle daily life events and ultimately decide on an action.

We are all human and in a physical world. I constantly remind myself of this and the fact that I am on a spiritual journey and not expected to get it right all the time. I also have learned that when I don't "get it right" not to let that set me back but instead learn from the mistake and use it as a contrast. My daily intention is to stay close to source and view events from its perspective. This ALWAYS brings clarity to the influence of my EGO and helps me adjust my actions to acquire my desired outcomes. The purposeful practice of allowing, in my opinion, is key to ensuring a lesson is effectively learned.

Lessons Learned:

*Remember, I am not limited in my potential to achieve my desires and manifest miracles in my life.

*Knowing I have forces seen and unseen on my side and they are always available to me guiding me and encouraging me to embrace my NOW power.

*Knowing that ALL of my physical experiences are divine and blessed for the greater good.

*Knowing that feelings of daily chaos are only a symptom of being out of alignment with source because, in a perfectly aligned universe, there is no chaos.

Through my life reflections, intentional focus, and starting to look at and understand my misguided understandings I have acquired tools for when life's challenges override my desired behavior or feelings towards any particular event presenting as overwhelming situations I may feel I can't overcome, then I act on my EGO's influence. I see in my constant changing now that each part of my journey has all been perfect and as it should be. It has ALL led me to an enlightenment and higher knowing. Those tools continue to guide and remind me how my perspective, thoughts, and beliefs regarding any person, thing, decision, or event directly affect the outcome of them.

I can tell you in my journey so far a BIG aha moment for me was when I realized I needed to be willing and open to looking at things a different way, including myself. When I began to do this on a regular basis, the things I looked at changed and I began to experience the miracles in my life "I" was manifesting through intentional focus and feeling. I have to share them and my new growing awareness of them including what changes I needed to make to I manifested them. In my book, I share personal lessons learned from deep self-reflection and from studying wisdom-sharing individuals also on a journey of abundance in their lives. The HOW is individual though so please realize that YOU have to unapologetically believe how powerful you are and YOU have to make the changes in your life to change your perspective. We have to learn to let go of the HOW. Take an honest look at yourself and your life. Most importantly be open-minded to what may seem impossible. My journey is relatable and through sharing it I hope to give you insight and support in knowing you too can grow and acquire your own desired outcomes. If you don't change what's not working and what keeps giving you the same result then how can you expect a different outcome? Stop living by anyone else's version of what they think your life should be. Start believing fiercely you CAN have whatever you want then actively live in that assumption.

I can promise you this, whatever you BELIEVE, you are right. If you believe you are a victim of circumstance then you are, if you believe you are strong, you are, if you believe you are alone, you are, if you believe you are eternally loved...you are. Your own life circumstances and events will prove this and they can be your guide to changing any part of it YOU decide to. It's a mindset. Start by asking yourself daily and often, Where is my focus? How am I FEELING? What do I WANT? Then listen for the answer. The answer to these questions will show you where you need to begin. You need to expect a change in your life if you want to achieve it. Don't forget to be YOU! I hope you are inspired by my book and my journey because I want you to, to feel the change that only you can bring to your life through intentional focus.

My ending thought, which I touch on throughout my book, is this: while doing this for yourself, always stop and think about how your actions or expectations of another are affecting their journey, both now and in the future. Remember how you've been affected throughout your life by others and their expectations of you and for YOUR life. Stop the cycle and, whenever you can, ALLOW.

Thank you for reading my story...

NOTE:

Be stubborn about making the changes you want to make
in your life for your best, most desired outcome.

Preface

Join me on a journey of self-realized lessons and newfound self-awareness. Discover with me how we manifest outcomes in our lives through our focus and beliefs. Through my studies of wise teachers like Wayne Dyer and Lao-tzu, The Tao-Te-Ching, an ancient text, as well as the Laws of Attraction I have developed a new enlightened mindset.

Follow me through the beginning of finding my power and letting go of the HOW. Begin to realize the same in your own life. Your life can change when you listen and learn by seeking out our ancient teachers and their wisdom. Be willing to change and refocus misguided understandings we have all experienced since birth.

If you enjoy Wayne Dyer's work, Neville Goddard, Greg Braiden, Ester Hicks, Ram Dass and other similar teachings you will enjoy reading how my life has changed through embracing and practicing their techniques of refocusing your subconscious mind and embracing your imagination to manifest through intentional focus.

Your power is in your now, and your desires are just waiting to be realized and manifested by you. With a willingness to open your mind, you might discover possibilities that you previously thought were unattainable.

Chapter One

<u>We All Have a Story</u>

Every individual has a unique narrative, deeply personal and wholly theirs. While we might share experiences with others, each of us navigates our journey from a distinct viewpoint, framed within the walls of our personal reality. The innermost thoughts, emotions, and reflections remain inaudible to others; they are ours and ours alone.

Life is an interplay of shared moments and solitary reflections. While we may walk side by side with others, our paths are our own, each marked by unique experiences and viewpoints. It's undeniable that every individual perceives the world differently. Narratives of the same event can vary drastically, colored by our personal lenses. My experiences have shown that while we all believe in our version of events, others might have contrasting perspectives. Often, disagreements are labeled as mere differences in opinion. Yet, more accurately, they are differences in perspective.

I began with that statement because I now realize that all of MY inner talk, worry, and perspective made my reality what it was. How I felt about any one thing or person, experience or decision were MY feelings derived from a belief system that was dictated to me. How could THAT be wrong? It was wrong because I was taught to worry about the future that was not even here yet, control the present that was never IN my control, and I always judged myself how I THOUGHT others perceived me even when I disagreed with what they had to say! and THAT became my identity and dictated perception. I was living by someone else's expectations of ME and it wasn't working. My mindset or EGO is very stealthy and usually assures me I was right and others were wrong. I now know this was my inner guidance system talking to me, but, I wasn't listening. Every one of us has a perspective but what we all forget is, just that, that OUR perspective is not the only one in the room. Dictated perspective is also present. We also forget to remember that, the only one that matters, when it is in regards to OURSELVES, is our own. We are not taught to listen to our own guidance system, rather we embrace the dictated perspectives and opinions of others as our own. I tried to live up to what I perceived as the person I was supposed to be. I tried to achieve the image that was acceptable, the house, kids, and job that was acceptable which made me miserable but I did not show it. I silently and internally just told myself that after each perceived failure, I would do better next time.

Perception is tricky, we all have one and we all insert it into our daily lives in almost every situation. We perceive what is best for ourselves we perceive how someone else meant something and we perceive what we think others perceive us as. I NEVER lived up to what in my mind I perceived to be the" me "I was SUPPOSED to be. I don't think I have to lay out every detail of my life raising three kids, and working from home so I could be there for them with a husband who worked day and night trying to provide everything HE perceived were the most important elements of what a good father does to provide for his family or trying to fit in at the PTA meetings, to paint this picture. I trust anyone reading this IS or HAS experienced what I am getting at. I bet reading this for some may be the first time of really realizing that we all have our own perspectives and expectations of ourselves that are derived from what we THINK others expect from us and think we should be like, believe in, care about or how we may just go about an event in our lives. From the time we are very young we are taught to believe who we ARE is what we are TOLD we should be. What I have come to KNOW now is that our perception of ourselves, when embraced through another's eyes or subjected to another's judgment, can lead to a loss of our true self. I now know that all I have to do is be myself. I don't have to "live up to" any version of what anyone else thinks I should be. Worrying about ANYTHING that MIGHT happen at some future date is giving up your power NOW. Living someone else's idea of your perfect life, perfect family, home, or job is

reaching for a promise of something that does not exist and giving up your life to an endless journey towards loss of self. As you read my book my hope is you see yourself and reflect on mostly YOU, your self-talk, and what YOU would like to acknowledge in and for your own life through sharing my personal experiences and lessons. I hope to inspire you to take a look at the way you interact, react or not, with your family, friends, kids, coworkers, or anyone else that comes into your experience. Remember that only those we invite into our journey can enter it. Your perception becomes your reality. This is an interesting concept and some will argue its legitimacy but the more you examine your day-to-day thoughts and feelings including your actions and focus, this fact will become very clear and undeniable.

We make and decide our reality all on our own. There is no one else to blame or hold responsible for ANYTHING in our journey. That will be a hard pill for most to swallow, I know it has been for me but it's getting easier as I realize how I took on a belief system that I had to be what I was told I had to be instead of becoming who I really am. I was living someone else's perception of what my life should be.

As I have taken a good hard honest look at my beliefs, perspective, self-image, focus, and mostly inner talk I have seen the difference in how I USED to feel about all the above and how I now know to.

Please join me while I continue my journey, to no destination but growing through intentional focus, self-observation, Spiritual

growth through new understandings of just HOW I get what I get in my life and beginning to understand why I may NOT yet have certain things in my life I desire including how my perception changes my reality and needs constant observation from me so it doesn't just dictate to me and keep me from being ME.

Chapter Two

MINDSET is PERSPECTIVE

For me, establishing a new mindset has been a progressive lesson. It happens in stages and at the most interesting times, it seems. Some lessons are learned the first time and others have had to be experienced over and over before the lesson actually sinks in. I have come to believe that noticing when things are not the way you "want" them to be is as important as being grateful when they are.

Staying stuck in the undesired is a choice. A choice in the sense that every time we complain, explain, elaborate, and share the undesired we perpetuate it and get more of it. Choosing to perpetuate by focusing on the direction of the problem keeps that momentum active and growing. So, what I have learned is..... change it. Change your words from what is NOT wanted to what IS wanted. Talk, imagine, elaborate, and share how you WANT it to be. Then, YOU have to believe it. BELIEVE your desires are already yours. Feeling how it would be and how your life would change if what you desire was already here is key to manifesting it. If you can't feel it, you don't believe it and cannot achieve it. To manifest your desires, you must see yourself living in the realization of that desire. It has to feel, to you, as if it's realistic for you to have or be what you desire.

You have to find a way to allow yourself to feel worthy too because you ARE. We are not raised to believe we can have or be anything we want to, a lot of times these desires are instead presented as limits we can not achieve. We end up believing someone else's version of what is possible and what we CAN or should have or do or be. We adopt the language of CAN'T instead of the perspective of I CAN.

FEEL THE DIFFERENCE

Adopt a new language. Feel the difference in what I was telling myself in this real example of simple self-talk.

ME: I don't want to go to work today, I have so much at home I need to do. I never have time for things I want to do. There are always chores and other responsibilities standing in the way of me getting to enjoy my life. All I do is work and clean the house.

<Vs>

ME: I am so grateful for my job. It is exactly what I asked for. I get to converse with all sorts of people, learn new things, and share my experiences. I am grateful for a husband who is my best friend and goes to work to support our family every day and with a

great attitude. I can't wait for the weekend to have some quiet time to myself and quality time with him.

When you aspire to a grateful attitude and simply change your mindset even the biggest challenges you face will ease and your perspective can become one of learning instead of strife.

This example can be applied to ANY negative self-talk about an undesired situation in our lives. Try it for yourself and feel the difference simply changing the words you use changes your mindset and how you feel and perceive. The difference in how you feel when you are grateful and choose happy over negative and defeated is profound and will change your life.

Clarity comes when we change the way we look at things. The clarity this lesson brings is personal. When you begin to listen to and pay attention to just how you are speaking regarding yourself and your life it will become very clear why you keep experiencing the undesired in your life and you begin to realize that just by changing your words your desired outcome will come much quicker.

We are not taught this and it takes practice. Be willing to learn and experience the process of changing your mindset and perspective. Remember, it's not a race or destination.

A PERSONAL AWAKENING

It was a warm day, sunny with a slight breeze. I left the house grabbing a notepad and pen on the way out the door. I got in the car and drove up the road to a very large field adjacent to a park. Leaving the kids and my husband at home, chores undone to go "get away" was not something I did on a regular basis or at all.

But I needed to, so I did. Leaving everyone and everything behind, I cleared my thoughts and for a short time, I sat on the grass, and broke out my pad and paper to start writing what ultimately would be the most honest feelings, concerns, self-doubt, and frustrations I had ever put to paper. It was a challenging time in my life and I didn't know what to do or, who to turn to. Writing down my thoughts and feelings began something inside of me that I had not experienced yet in my life. A feeling of clarity and self-empowerment.

I felt "safe" writing them down. I would never speak them out loud because I am not a confrontational person and at this point in my life, was not strong enough in my truth to express myself. I have always been more of a go-along-to-get-along person. In writing, I felt safe. I could write anything I wanted to about anyone or anything that was on my mind without conflict, opinion, or consequence. It was amazing.

I suddenly felt lighter and had clarity about what I needed to do but I still needed to work on believing I could do it. I had an instant feeling of positive forward motion and a new attitude about what I had been challenged with. I could see that how I was speaking and how I felt regarding events and people in my life was exactly, how things were playing out.

After going back and reading what I had written it was all so clear to me. My perception was my reality but I was creating it, my thoughts regarding certain people and situations were exactly

how I had decided the facts were and they became the situations I could not see my way past because I was literally stuck in my perception with EGO as my guide creating my undesired reality. Reading my words was very enlightening and I began to realize my mindset was not working in my favor.

I now believe this was the point I began to realize that I was the attractor of my reality. I asked myself "Can it be that simple?'

Knowing what to do and believing it can be done are very different and as I soon realized, would be the hardest part. This is the learning curve I feel we all have to deal with. Believing, believing that what we want, what we deserve, and what we need to do to get it is possible and it's OK to pursue.

Sometimes the lesson is learned the first time, sometimes, it takes longer. The years to come showed me in so many ways how easy it can be to change your reality, and as hard as I made it. It was still many years from this awakening that I really began to understand and listen to my inner voice. It took time to overcome how I usually dealt with conflict or emotions in general not to mention my own self-doubt and image. It took time to be strong enough to stand in my own truth.

Through writing my thoughts out I had the opportunity to take an honest look at what is really going on in my head and in any given situation. It provided clarity and has proven to me what is sometimes hard to understand when I am "in my head". It helps me get out of my own way.

Every time I write, it comes from a very strong inspiration. I can literally hear someone clearly speaking to me and my brain can't stop, like a stenographer typing a dictation with no pause. In the end, I always feel so clear and calm. The calm brings clarity, the clarity brings focus, and my focus, now on my desires and true feelings, acquire my desires with no action from me. I highly recommend doing this yourself. Write down what you are truly struggling with, how you truly feel, and what you really desire for your life. You don't have to share it with anyone. Go back and read it often especially when you notice a shift in your mindset and a change in your life in regards to circumstances or unexpected miracles. Be sure to date your writings and absolutely be sure to write about any changes you desired that you have now acquired noting thoughts on how you made that change manifest. The HOW is divine, we bring it through letting go of control and faith that source knows the best HOW and the best when.

Waiting can be the hardest part, we want what we want when we want it. For myself, I have come to realize, so many times that MY time is NOT necessarily the best time for my desires to manifest. I now say thank you for the "waiting" and acknowledge the amazing and beautiful ways my desires have manifested for me when I am patient.

They come in ways that I could not have possibly, brought about myself. I now ENJOY and embrace the waiting KNOWING that when I get my desire and it manifests into reality it will be better than I could have ever imagined and always, at the PERFECT time. I believe that when we live in the end and use our imagination to experience our desires ahead of the manifestation experiencing the feeling of REALITY we can be sure our desire is on its way.

When I say I literally heard someone speaking to me I don't mean like I hear voices, I mean I hear myself very clearly telling myself what I knew but was for some reason not listening to before. I believe we all do this and that the "voice" is our non-physical selves teaching us if we choose and are willing to listen. I feel so inspired at these times when my non-physical self brings me the most beautiful clarity I couldn't find before.

We all have a non-physical self, and we have all heard it when it tries to speak to us. That voice in your head telling you one thing and you do another, then say, "I knew I should have..." I also realize that the more I learn the more I realize that "learning" will be my most constant companion. It truly is the journey NOT the destination that matters. As soon as you get where you think you need to be or must be or should be you will find and eventually learn, that it is not where you will or want to stay. We are ever-changing and will never "be finished."

So the lessons continue and so does life.

While revisiting my notebooks I originally paused when I thought about sharing my thoughts and lessons. I asked myself if they could benefit anyone else as this would be the only reason I could think of to share them. I believe and have come to know what I have felt, dealt with, accepted, realized, and learned through the years IS valuable and mostly, relatable. I hope anyone who reads my words feels and realizes they are not alone. We are all individually powerful beings with the free will to manifest our every desire. All we have to do is realize it, believe it, FEEL it, and accept that it is already ours by living as though it is. This realization does not happen overnight and it does not happen without intentional focus and change. Each one of us has to decide for ourselves where we want our lives to go. I also encourage you to seek out and listen to others who have amazing insight and perspective in this journey of change. A few I have learned tremendously from and respect immensely are:

Wayne Dyer
Ester Hicks (Abraham)
The Tao De Ching
Neville Goddard and
Ram Daas

As we individually set out on our journeys towards personal enlightenment, it is important to remember that allowing others their lessons, desires, self, beliefs, and life is a very important lesson, and, the one that may take the longest to master. Touching back on individual perspectives for a moment, I feel it is important to remember everyone will hear and interpret things a little differently from each other. Instead of thinking you need to correct another on their understanding, listen and thank them for sharing because you may just learn something. Sharing is love and dictating is control. When sharing your perspective, it's important to remember this distinction. Share to uplift and be of service, not to dictate and expect another to bend to your will or be as you expect they should be.

Note: The way to abundance is by adopting a mindset of flow.

Chapter Three

MISGUIDED UNDERSTANDINGS

Childhood to Adulthood

Family dynamics, child rearing, our social lives and style, habits and desires change as we grow up from what others have influenced us into thinking they should be to what WE desire and want them to be, or, they don't then we blame the ones that influenced our lives growing up for where our lives are at and how they turned out taking no responsibility for our circumstances.

This is an example of one of MY misguided understandings... On a warm spring morning, I got up early to fix breakfast before getting everyone off to school and work. The front window was open and a perfectly cool morning breeze was flowing through the house.

I could hear the kids getting up and figuring out the bathroom dynamics as they got ready for school. My husband was back and forth to the car getting it packed with the things he needed for his day.

I finished cooking breakfast and kept it warm on the stove for anyone who may have time to even realize it was there. To me, this was something that a good mom does that loves her family as my mom did the same for my brothers and me when we were young.

I enjoyed doing things that I perceived, made my family feel special and that were done out of my love for them. In the moment I was focused on the tasks at hand, feeding everyone, encouraging focus on getting out the door on time, breaking up engagements of opinions regarding who takes too long in the bathroom always making the other late, and trying to be on everyone's "Side" but still keep the peace.

As anticipations of the day ahead were on everyone's minds my goal, again what I perceived a "good" mom does was to KNOW those anticipations and ease them. It felt like the best way to do that was to take care of the issues myself as opposed to letting them figure it out for themselves which meant they may suffer a consequence.

My misguided understanding and action here was I was more than willing and felt it my duty to suffer that consequence myself instead of allowing the lesson. This is how I was raised, I was "taken care of" I was not allowed to make a decision because, after all, I was just a child. Right?

I was raised to depend on others to fix things for me, to tell me what I wanted and how I should act, what I could like or dislike or believe. So I embraced this as the way a good parent teaches their children. Dictate to them their desires, abilities, and beliefs including dealing with any hardship that may bestow upon them regarding a choice they made. These misguided understandings were the beginning of my early life's development and misguided understandings of self that shaped who I was and would grow up to be. If I had been shown self-worth, strength, and ability instead, I would have been more prepared for real life which would have served me better along the road of my true desires. My parents, as most parents, did what they knew to do. I now understand that they raised me out of love. However, if we simply follow the same path because someone else took it, and don't consider changing our approach—especially when it directly impacts another— then complaining about the method and outcome becomes just an automatic response rooted in a misguided understanding.

I was always told and expected to accept that it is the adult's responsibility to dictate the child's thoughts and actions when the opposite is true. No one should dictate another's actions or beliefs even as a child. Children become dependent on direction then they resent it then they look for it. Demonstrating and supporting from an early age, a child's own ability to influence a desired outcome through the concept and reality of a consequence is an invaluable lesson most are denied due to misguided understandings and expectations carried forward from one's own childhood.

So, the question is, whose fault is it that I felt like "I" had to suffer a consequence under the excuse of protecting my kids from one? or what my understanding of an adult's role is? My parents and those who influenced my younger years? That's the easy way out for sure and definitely a misguided understanding. Blaming them and taking no responsibility for my own life and actions is ANOTHER consequence of a misguided understanding. They influenced me but for me to BLAME them for making the choices I make is wrong.

Take a moment here and reflect back on whose belief system YOU may be embracing and blaming for your life situations. We are in control of our own lives and to say differently is giving your own power away. Take it back!

Instead of blaming, seeing the contrast between the unwanted to the wanted is a much better way to move forward making the changes in your own life that you feel best serve you and your desires. If we get stuck and don't know how to handle or move forward with a situation, paying close attention to how you FEEL regarding it and any course of action you are considering is a great place to start. The way you FEEL is a great guide to the correct action to take. It may contradict how you THINK is the best course of action but what I have come to know is, in the long run, when I follow how I feel, not emotionally feel but gut feel, I am rarely disappointed with my choice. How often have you ignored that "gut" feeling and then wished you would have listened?

My Misguided Understandings here were:

*Trying to be everyone's friend

*My perception of what a "good mom" was taking care of everything instead of allowing the lesson and the difference between protecting and supporting vs teaching and empowering.

But mostly, as I got to be an adult, I thought that my actions, thoughts, beliefs, decisions, or desires that brought my undesired reality were ANYONE else's fault.

If I Knew Then What I Know Now

I would have encouraged refocus and deliberately creating one's desired outcome. I would have encouraged a more independent, personal focus on what exactly each person desired as an outcome instead of trying to control it and thinking by doing so I was protecting them in some way. I did not understand the Universal Laws at that stage of my experience as I do now.

Reflecting Back

I look back and smile.

It is like a movie that plays in perfect step with life. We learn and change as we go, it is the way of our ever-growing and expanding beings. I can see in my constant changing now, that each part of my journey was all as it should be. It has all led me to an enlightenment and higher knowing today.

Even though I can look back on these now-learned lessons and be grateful for them I do know the impact "I" had and I DO wish I could go back with the wisdom learned and reteach. But, I also understand and do not blame myself for any misguided understandings I may have passed on because, just like the ones that influenced me, I had to learn the lesson first. What I now know and can do is live my truth by example remembering that dictating my now-learned lessons will not teach them to another. This big lesson is one I hope to share in my book and start a conversation around by starting to realize our misguided understandings and begin to change the understandings we all have regarding them.

With my knowing of all of this I like to believe that my family, no matter what, knows I would always be there for them and my INTENTIONS were from my heart and in their best interest ...as I knew them to be at the time. I now focus on living the example instead of dictating to others what their path, desires, beliefs, or wants should be.

I have learned and continue to realize that we will all have times of clarity, seeing how the people who raised us and their misguided understandings that lead them in their influences on us, affect us in our current lives and we will all learn something along our journeys from them. Hopefully not blame them but in our hearts be grateful for them because without the contrast of their lessons, how could we realize our own and change the narrative?

Forgiving someone for doing their best, the best they knew at any given time, for you, and recognizing YOU can change the effect THEIR misguided understandings may have had in your life is the beginning of learning to allow. Move forward in your own life and realize you too, WILL experience your own misguided understandings and most likely, affect another's life in the process. This is part of our journeys and is actually a very good learning tool for the affected and the inflictor.

Leave the blame game behind and realize that was their journey and you got the benefit of their hard lessons. You ARE in control of your life and the choices you make. Don't blame another for your understandings that become your misguided understandings. Change the story. You are powerful and in control. We cannot go back but we can humbly move forward in the knowing and pay the wisdom forward when the opportunity comes along. Ask yourself this, if someone treated you in any way that made you feel badly or that influenced your life so much that their undesired behavior carried forward into your own life, then why would you continue it? and do the same to another all the while complaining about it being done to you. Just because you were "wronged" does not give you the right to do it to another. Changing it and doing it differently will begin a deep healing in the way an unwanted event of the past affects you in your future.

Change it.

Chapter Four

<u>A Tricky Lesson</u>

Learning how to allow and not control could be considered a misguided understanding part 2. We are taught from childhood that adults are the boss and however they want us to behave and feel about something is for our own good. We adopt and accept false ideas of ourselves which creates the rebellion and inner conflict that leads to a path away from who we really are. Rarely do parents consider allowing a child to have an opinion let alone ask them what it may be because this is just not, how they were raised.

Allowing one to express themselves regardless of age is a very interesting concept but I feel often unthinkable to most parents. This could be considered a lot of people's first experience with a misguided understanding realized.

There is a fine line between "Take care of" and "Control or Guide"

Take care of = Assist

Guide = Listen and Live or, be the example

Control = Dictate and have expectations of or for another

Most of us were raised under the CONTROL example to some extent or another.

As a parent myself, I understand that there are boundaries and it IS up to us to guide our children, but most of us were not taught to GUIDE, we were shown to DICTATE.

I feel that treating children and young people with respect and giving them a voice is a very beneficial experience for them, and I believe for the parents as well. The saying, from the mouth of babes, comes to mind. If one thinks that just because we are older we cannot possibly learn from listening to a child's "opinion" or idea has a lot to learn for sure. Reflecting back on your own experiences with this is your best teacher. Not being heard or being allowed to have a voice is something that follows you into adulthood. This is definitely an area we can all work on to not perpetuate. I have grown into this mindset myself, I cannot say I practiced it as a young parent but I can say I see the wisdom in it now. Even if you don't have children, dictating to another is just better left out of the equation.

As children, we have a clear understanding of source and our inner guidance system. Then as we grow up we are influenced by others who tell us we are wrong and must follow their understandings.

We came into this life experience by choice, to expand the whole and learn. As we grow and are influenced by our life experiences some never get back to their own knowing as some are blessed to continue to discover it or, rediscover it as the years go by.

Life happens, aha moments teach us, days end and new ones always give us another opportunity to get closer to what we

"Know" and not follow what we have been told we HAVE to "Know" and do.

I myself constantly evaluate the child-raising years and ask myself "Were you being protective and supportive or selfish and controlling? My intention was to protect, teach, love, and support. The saying the road to heaven is paved with good intentions helps my EGO feel better but I know that just because one "means" well does not mean it is well meant or, the best action. Even though my intentions were to protect, teach love, and support, they were not always interpreted that way. I now see that because those I was influencing, pushed back as I dictated my misguided understanding into their journey. I do not blame the ones who have influenced me nor do I blame myself for my undesirable influence on others through the years. Instead, I recognize both and proceed with a fresh understanding of my own power to control and acquire what I want in my life, and I remember to allow others the same.

I have come to understand that my job is to be MY authentic self and an inspiration by living my truth, to inspire by allowing others their selves and journey, and to always, listen to the children, listen to my inner voice, and never tell another what their truth is or should be. If we remember our inner guidance system that we all came here with and truly listen to it, it will guide us through the learning curve of misguided understandings. This leads us to a desired outcome, showing that the real lesson is in 'allowing'. By embracing this, we recognize our misguided understandings and journey towards inner growth.

Allowing brings us inner peace and growth.

At the end of a hard workday, coming home to notes from a teacher about no homework turned in, again, hurt feelings over rejection at school, laundry backing up, trying to lose weight again, and your significant other stressed because the boss at work is a jerk all lend to no time for learning how to "allow". It is all out survival mode, yours and every member of the family that you are responsible for. Where do you even start to find the energy to ALLOW??? let alone teach it by example when all you want to do is go hide under the covers.

How? Intentional Focus.

When children especially are involved who literally have no clue about the stress of a job and supporting a family bringing a complete expectation that their issues trump ours leads us to actions of reaction and the children often respond in kind. At this point, no communication is going to be productive. Until children grow up and have adult responsibilities, they can't fully understand why you did or did not do what in their young minds was SO bad and unfair.

How I responded to these stresses was out of love and the desire for everyone to feel important, relevant, and heard but as I have stated previously, that is not always how it was perceived. I now see my responses more as EGO, desperation, and again, misguided understandings of how to get what I wanted through intentional focus and creation.

Allowing is not just letting others be themselves or make their own choices but rather having no negative opinions or emotions about those choices. Having negative emotions regarding another's choices is only tolerating and tolerating involves opinion and opinions are like anything else unpleasant or unwanted. Allowing is not just something we need to do for others, it is equally important to do for ourselves. Allow yourself to feel as you do and want what you genuinely want. When you don't "do it right" or "lose it," give yourself a break. The key is to notice these moments and immediately change your direction. Lessons learned will always be our biggest teachers.

I have always "heard" and felt my emotional guidance system but as I have gotten older, I have begun to understand it and listen to it. I have learned that my focus is what I need to watch because whatever IT is, on is what I am manifesting to be my reality. As a parent, it never sat well with me to have strong opinions about what one of my kids chose to wear, do, not do, say, or believe, especially if it led to conflict with them. It always ended with hurt feelings, rolled eyes, and distance between us. I had never known about, or even heard of, 'allowing' or focusing on a desired outcome (intentional focus). So, I didn't have the tools to teach it, either by example or otherwise. Trying to explain to my children what I, as an adult, experience and confront daily seemed nearly impossible, and I've come to realize it was misguided. The times I would attempt it, my words went in one ear and out the other, and when these two worlds collided a "When I was a kid" statement came up in the hopes of getting them to understand why I was so impatient and stressed just made the entire experience worse.

This is called communication breakdown. No matter what you go through in your day it cannot even be taken into consideration during those oh-so-stressful conversations where everything wrong in their world is our fault and they can not possibly understand what is going on in yours. Then no matter how that conversation ends the parent feels inadequate and the child feels unimportant. My focus being on controlling an outcome instead of allowing, communication and mutual respect brought me exactly what I was focused on and GETTING, conflict.

Definity, not peace.

Interesting when you stop and realize how similar the emotions are and where they stem from, right? We were not taught allowing or communication skills so when it became my turn to parent, the misguided understandings continued and were passed on. Allowing the children to make a decision that was the opposite of what I knew was best for them under the "I was raised to" mentality continued the exact same experience I had when it was done to me.

I rarely if ever even asked my kids what they thought or how they felt about something. I feel this misguided understanding that was so natural to me is what brought me a lot of inner turmoil and self-doubt. I did not recognize that, as my inner guidance I just recognized it as the children fighting me and me taking control. I am in no way saying to just let children run amuck and always do as they please but instead taking into account what they feel regarding a situation or decision that involves them is worth considering. This can be the beginning or starting point of YOUR intentional focus lesson and a personal lesson for them instead of a dictated decision by you.

It IS our job as parents to guide them so if after they express their thoughts you still need to take the lead then at least do it in a teaching way that leaves the child feeling valued and heard. They will learn to do the same and most likely will learn from what you ultimately decide is the best decision. This leads to less negative emotions about your decision and will begin to show by example, what it means to allow.

I talk about the children in this example because if we want to change the pattern of continued misguided understandings being embraced through the generations, we need to start with the children and their knowing and feelings. Allowing them to have a voice will teach them respect and critical thinking including consequences to be considered when making a decision as opposed to emotional choices.

I feel this practice is a good one to embrace when interacting with other family members, co-workers, spouses, siblings, or anyone else in your life as well. It can be beneficial to do things differently than you may have before in regards to, say a sibling that you love but don't really like much which has led to feelings of resentment. Try to have a conversation with them where you are not defending yourself, views, or explaining why this or why that. Just listen to them, hear them, and try to see things from their perspective not having to be "right" or heard yourself at that particular moment. This allows them to feel heard, offers you perspectives you might not have had before, and cultivates the art of listening, caring, and allowing in both parties. It is truly an eye-opening exercise when achieved.

Getting out of our own way, and being open to hearing someone else's account of an event can teach us a lot. It doesn't mean you have to agree on everything, but you can likely find common ground to respectfully disagree and transition from past negative emotions to a place of allowing and greater acceptance.

Try listening more than sharing. People want to be heard not dictated to. Wouldn't you agree that sometimes, just being able to voice something that's on your mind or bothering you, all of a sudden gives you a new perspective on the issue? I have had that experience many times so, for me, I prefer listening to sharing and then asking, "Which direction FEELS best to you?" by asking someone that can help them evaluate the decision from a feeling standpoint instead of an emotion or fear-based one. I practice this for myself as well and is definitely a lesson learned for me that guides me and never fails me.

Change the misguided understanding progression and listen don't just control all the time. When we are tired and need to get things done it SEEMS easier to just control everything because we think there is no time to allow or listen. But if you do this as an intentional focus exercise, watch how things will begin to fall into place and the ones you are trying to take care of and communicate with will change their reactions and emotional responses. Something Wayne Dyer says is: "when we change the way we look at things the things we look at change" that includes our actions.

Intentional focus, allowing ourselves and others as opposed to what we all usually lean on, emotional reactive responses, is one way to change the direction of an outcome from an undesired to a desired one.

Chapter Five

Be the student

You may be wondering as you're reading my book where these ideas and 'knowing's' I refer to actually came from. Well, it started the day I was led to begin writing.

It has developed through many years and many realizations as I began to study the Law Of Attraction. I began to purposely manifest and notice when it happened, which created a desire to continue and a calling to acknowledge what I always felt but didn't know. When I let go of controlling the HOW, the floodgates opened, and my life became a series of miracles. Sometimes you don't know what your focus will ultimately bring, but if it is on your desires, the surprise of the HOW is incredible.

Remembering to live in a state of gratefulness every day keeps my mindset aligned with my desires. If I have judgment or criticism towards another, I focus on sending them love because I believe that no matter how much my human self tries to convince me I am right to have those emotions, I KNOW that if I am not in a state of love, I cannot acquire my wishes of living a divine life, close to source. I strive to love all people as source loves them. I am no saint, I am learning and have a strong desire to do what makes me feel good in my soul and not give in to what makes me feel frustrated, angry, sad, or critical. I believe that if you want to accomplish something for yourself you first have to see yourself in that role or as that person.

The law of Attraction is always at work. You can believe it or choose not to believe it. It doesn't matter, the choice is yours. I can tell you though, that when you consider and begin to live on purpose, acknowledging the law of attraction and how it is working in your life you begin to understand just how powerful you are and the power you have over what you are getting in your journey, or not getting for that matter. This is what changed my life and drove me to share my experiences. I want to inspire others to listen to their inner voice and change misguided understandings by altering their own perspectives. Realize that others are not your job, you are your job. These are all lessons I have learned including continuing to ask myself what abundance is to me and then working towards it.

It took a big aha moment before I could look back and realize that what was manifesting in my life, I had been very, fiercely focused on and that I was creating without intention. When I realized this and learned how to create by intentional focus my entire life path changed. I now know that mindset is the key so I work every day to keep mine focused on my new belief system letting the dictated one go. Growing in love and inspiration remembering to live by example and not judgment.

As I have studied, opened my mind, and learned to take an honest look at myself, my thoughts, my self-image, and talk I also began to understand and practice(and it does take practice!) the art of allowing. It started to become very obvious to me that when I was trying to control an outcome either for myself or someone else my opinions and judgments around it were what was causing me so much stress. Now, the practice of the art of allowing is a tool I use all the time and I have to say, it is a constant lesson and intentional act but still not always an easy one. It is getting easier as I recognize the benefits of it for myself and the people in my life. It has improved relationships and given me a personal sense of peace.

I feel strongly about sharing this tool with parents. Parenting is the hardest job anyone could ever endure. It's the most important and profound experience that will take you on a journey of self-doubt, the ultimate love of another human being, and put you in situations of judgment and need to control as you have never experienced before. You will never feel more out of control and lost doing anything else in your life.

When children learn early how to deal with struggles, allow others, and in addition recognize when their focus is in the wrong place, on the wrong thing, and how to redirection their inner talk back to what they want and not on what is wrong or undesirable sets them on a path of fulfillment and inner peace. Changing the misguided understandings of our youth can set our children on a new path of self-love and empowerment. I have often reflected back on my child-raising years and learned so much about myself. These years have made me stronger today and taught me invaluable lessons I now enjoy sharing with parents while supporting them in their parent journey. Because I have experienced it I can speak to it and that is how I know that when I talk about teaching your children love, self-reliance, allowing, and giving them the tools to acquire their desires by intentional focus, I am speaking from a point of experience and contrast. A new generation is in your hands; it is worth the time to invest in yourself, live the example, show humility, and stay open to what you may think is impossible so you can show your children and others in your life the amazing power we all have as unlimited beings.

There is no destination here, to reach. We will always be learning and striving to live our best life. We will fall short and we will also soar! If we don't fail how will we know when we accomplish? If we never have mountains to climb and challenges to overcome, how can we understand the strength, love, and power we possess? We have to believe in ourselves no matter what or none of this matters. You cannot access the life you want with a negative outlook or belief system. You're not in a race, it's your journey.

This is why your judgments on another whether it is your child, parent, spouse, or friend are misplaced. All we have to do is concentrate on our own house, our own life, and lessons, or we cannot be free. If you are judging another you are not focused on yourself and your growth. Look at yourself and your habits that may need to change for your own enlightenment. This was another focus I had to learn because I needed to change it. I needed to learn practices of self-focus, letting go of worry and control over others or situations I felt only I could handle for the proper outcome.

Remember, this is a practiced skill. All this is, we are not naturally good at it. It takes commitment and work. We learn a lot during childhood through adulthood that we need to unlearn and take a close look at. We need to be able to be patient with ourselves, quiet our minds, and seek clarity. Ask for what you want and learn to wait for it. You get better as you practice self-awareness and love for others, allowing an intentional focus.

A big lesson I learned happened when I asked that question: what do I have to unload and relearn? I had to learn to allow questions without an answer, and then wait for the response of the universe to bring me the teachers I needed. I had to be willing to wait and trust that the answers I need will come and the situations I desire will manifest.

I had to take a look at my perception of what I thought the right decision was too. I realized that when I make a bad decision there are a lot of noises in my head as opposed to a quite calm feeling I get when I make the right choice. I have learned to ask "What am I not seeing?" The universe hears how we feel not what we say, so when I began to realize the answers to these questions were there all the time being brought to me through my inner guidance system and my words and feelings were what was not aligned, I changed them.

Then, the people and situations I had asked for just started to come to me, manifesting in the most perfect amazing ways.

Teachers and guides, answers, and opportunities became abundant.

Don't be so attached to your own ideas that you're not open to change. You have the power to change your life. You are responsible for your journey and the creator of your life. Acknowledging this and that it is no one else's responsibility but yours to change your life in the direction of your desired outcomes sets you on a path to FEEL your power and know you are in control.

Chapter Six

Let go of what isn't working

In conclusion: I would just like to say that my journey of realizing how strong I am, how I AM in control of my life and my mindset is the key to my desired path could not have been possible without acquiescing and beginning to listen to others' wisdom, guidance, and insight. Realizing my own misguided understandings and working every day not to perpetuate them has been one of my biggest lessons.

We have to be willing to take an honest look at our own lives before we can embrace positive change, seeing ourselves living our desires.

My teachers, who range from Wayne Dyer, Ram Dass, Neville Goddard, and Ester Hicks to name a few, have been key in helping me realize that all I have to do is be happy. This may sound trite, but I have come to embrace the essence of their messages and in my own life begin to practice them.

I don't practice self-pity or blame anymore and have become strong in my truth. I do not need to change anyone else's mind but enjoy sharing my new belief system with like-minded people who continue to teach me that none of us will ever get it right all the time, nor are we meant to. I embrace my challenges and aspire to see them for what they are, a learning opportunity. My challenges teach me that I am responsible for myself and not for anyone else. It is not up to me to change another or expect them to do it my way.

I am not without my human weaknesses and I still judge and have an opinion but now, I quickly feel the feeling of how judging another "feels" which quickly reminds me I have plenty in my own life "house" to work on, I don't need to work on someone else's.

Love and listen to the children, remember when you were a child, do it differently when you need to stop a misguided understanding, and teach with love and respect to create new understandings. Empower the children so they grow up knowing their own power and put them on a path of self-awareness and love.

When you feel the need or catch yourself dictating to another, stop for a moment and change your direction. Consider listening and allowing even if you feel you know what that decision may mean for that person. YOU cannot teach them life lessons that will show them their truth by imposing your own opinion on them. Nor should you allow another to do this to you.

Live the example of what you want to express. Change your own life and live in service for others with no expectation of anything back. This can be a smile, a conversation with someone who may be lonely or just not responding back to a negative act towards you.

You don't have to be right all the time. You don't have to speak or defend all the time. You don't have to control everything even when it feels like if you don't, no one will.

Quiet your mind, say thank you for your challenges, and be grateful for your blessings. Just, be happy.

This is my first book and I want to thank you for reading it. My hope is that my experiences, new belief systems, and practices of positive self-awareness illustrate to you that we can all change, it's okay to be you and listen to your inner voice. I didn't realize I was on a journey until I came to the end of my road and chose a new road that has put me on a new path and journey of love. When I stopped and realized I am more than I was taught growing up and embraced my knowing realizing how powerful and relevant I am the strength and clarity that came were undeniable.

Every moment, every lost job, lost friend, or heartache including all perceived failures, are individual journeys and WE are in control of ours. The Law of Attraction is at work always, believe it or not. Every journey is a personal one so remember, pay attention to yours and don't dictate another's. Learn from each other and see every person as a part of God and the whole, just different but no less than another.

No one else is responsible for your choices or your life so be strong and stand in your truth allowing others to do the same.

With no judgment, we are all unique divine beings. Lastly, give yourself a break; perfection isn't always attainable since we exist in a physical, human world. The critical aspect is recognizing when you're veering into negative patterns and consciously choosing to shift your perspective.

Begin anywhere, and remember to embrace and love yourself because you are deeply loved!

Inspirational Quotes

"I have been all things unholy; if God can work through me, he can work through anyone." -ST. FRANCIS OF ASSISI

"Do not feel lonely; the entire universe is inside you." -RUMI

"You are the sole architect of your reality. Nobody else can shape your life the way you do. It's all you, in every nuance and detail. Focus less on externalities, and let your imagination soar." -ESTER HICKS

"Life gracefully dances between the art of holding on and the freedom of letting go." –RUMI

In the last pages of my book I wanted to share some of the simple, so true and very insightful words from inspirational people that I admire very much as a huge thank you to them all.

WAYNE DYER

"How people treat you is their karma; how you react is yours...."

"It makes no sense to worry about things you have no control over because there's nothing you can do about them, and why worry about things you do control?"

"Until you transcend the ego, you can do nothing but add to the insanity of the world. When you're connected to the power of intention, everywhere you go, and everyone you meet, is affected by you and the energy you radiate."

"Judgements prevent us from seeing the good that lies beyond appearances"

"Abundance is not something we acquire. It is something we tune into."

"The highest form of ignorance is when you reject something you don't know anything about"

NEVILLE GODDARD

"Do not waste time in regret."

"Change your conception and you will change the world."

"The world is a mirror."

"All things evolve out of consciousness."

"All you can possibly need or desire is already yours."

Some of the best quotes of all time…..

"You must be the change you wish to see in the world."

— Mahatma Gandhi

"Find out who you are and do it on purpose."

— Dolly Parton

"The only thing we have to fear is fear itself"

— Franklin D Roosevelt

"Do one thing every day that scares you."

— Eleanor Roosevelt

"Well done is better than well said."

— Benjamin Franklin

Doing our best every day to stay positive applying all the inspirational messages we can in our daily desire to be happy, passing on and living the example while learning to allow ourselves and others the time and grace to not always get it right, we must not give up. If we give up, what's the point?

Why give up when there is so much more to learn and experience? If something in your life is not working and you're not happy examine that reality and make the changes necessary to live your best life.

Every day I get up, the first thing I say is thank you for being given another chance to love, be loved and experience this amazing journey I have been blessed with.

Seek out your truth and others that can support and assist you in finding it.

Much love — A Student of Satori

JUST SAY THANK YOU

BE GRATFUL

BE HAPPY

LOVE YOURSELF

ALLOW

TAKE THE TIME TO MAKE THE CHANGES

SUMMING IT UP

In summary of this book, here are some key things to remember and focus on when you partake on your own individual journey of spiritual growth.

* Write it down honestly.

What would you like to intentionally attract into your life? What would you like to change that is not working?

Then, be passionately aware and fiercely focused on the answer to those questions believe you can make them and take the steps necessary to manifest them.

*See yourself as you want to be.

Visualize that dream job, house or car. Feel the feeling of the relationship you have wanted for so long fulfills you. See yourself successfully writing the perfect paper for a school assignment. Attract what you WANT not more of what you don't want or what someone else thinks is best for you.

*Remember-

Thoughts attract other "like" thoughts so stop the negative self-talk and spoken word about the undesired. To change your life you have to change the way you think and feel. Understand the power of your THOUGHTS.

*Expect it!

Expect what you want to come and put no expectation of time on it. The timing is not yours to control or know. We often are impatient when there is an urgent need or want but if you trust in the universe to know the absolute perfect timing for everything and the HOW you will be AMAZED by the results of your faith. You do not need to control the HOW. Believe you deserve your desire and see yourself in the end result. The only help the universe needs from you is your unwavering faith and KNOW it is yours.

*Don't get caught up in drama.

Pay attention to who is pulling you into a negative space or keeping you in a belief system that feels wrong to you. You will KNOW if your actions are self-serving or, serving yourself. If you are not fulfilling YOUR inner knowing it is ok to change course and do what is best for you. Remember, your job is YOU, so pay attention to what you are allowing into your experience.

By doing this you are helping others too because getting caught up in drama, someone else's negative talk or thoughts is only perpetuating that situation for them and affecting you at the same time. It only assists in their miss-creating and assists them manifesting into their life more of what they do not want.

If someone else wants to complain and perpetuate sickness, undesired outcomes or the same bad life situations they have always received – Let them.

Love them and don't judge them. They are on their own journey and it is their choice not yours to do for themselves what THEY feel. Just don't stick around or participate in the miss-creating and take a chance of their situation starting up your negative talk and feelings.

*Help others and be a service to them by living the example of your desired life. Live YOUR truth and show them instead of tell or dictate to them how focusing on positive changes, learning to hear and listen to your inner voice and guidance system is how you hear source, find your power and acquire the strength to make the needed changes in your life.

*If what you are asking for feels wrong,

If you don't believe….you can have it or deserve it, you will not. You cannot manifest something you do not believe is yours or that you deserve.

*Change takes consistent attention, time and focus. You must be patient with yourself but vigilant. Ask yourself tough questions being honest in your answers regarding your own habits and behavior.

This is a conversation only you can hear and answers only you can give. You need to continuously look inside yourself to evaluate what habits and thoughts need extermination. Get rid of the old so the new can come in.

It is imperative to be honest with yourself if you are going to make positive, hard choices and move towards a new mindset and belief system including hearing your inner voice and knowing the difference when EGO pops in.

*Only when you recognize what actions, thoughts and habits bring you the undesired will you be free. You must absolutely, once and for all stop the continued behavior that is not allowing you to grow and live your truth by becoming your authentic self.

* As you begin to make changes in your life remember this:

Stop judging and seeing all the faults others have. Instead, acknowledge those flaws in yourself. Realize you probably cut people off too, or give a look you did not intend to be offensive to someone else, or say something that is hurtful when you were just trying to help.

We ALL have flaws, bad habits, hurtful ways and habits we just can't seem to kick. So, work on you. What you're irritated about in another you are most likely doing yourself.

Look inside, make the changes there and stop looking outside. You have enough to do with your own growth, don't get distracted trying to fix someone else.

*We will never be done. We are not a piece of furniture that one day, will be all put together perfectly. We will always have more to learn, more to change and work on and always more growing to embrace. Be humble, be love, be kind and remember to forgive. Forgive yourself when you don't "get it right" or fall back into old habits. Recognizing when you do is more important than beating yourself up for it.

Forgive others for the same. Support others when they fall and give yourself a break when you, in a moment are not strong. Without challenges, trials and pain there cannot be growth or clarity. Be patient for the answers you seek and open your heart to hear them when they come.

We are all on a journey with no destination. Expanding our spirituality and experiencing this human, physical life with all of its blessings.

*Stop perpetuating misguided understandings.

We have all experienced misguided understandings and we all pass them on. They are usually experienced by default and passed down through the generations with the understanding, or excuse, "That's how I was raised"

The ones I focus on in my book relate to dictating another's belief system, what someone else thinks is best for their own life as opposed to what is expected of them and basic dictating to anyone else who they should be or how they should feel.

Misguided understandings come in all forms and disguise. We are all guilty of continuing them and inflicting them on our own children, husbands, friends and even ourselves. It doesn't matter if we were affected positively or negatively by them.

Acknowledging them and working on a new direction is part of what we all need to include in our new belief system moving forward towards our desired outcomes.

*You are infinitely and unconditionally loved. You have a support system that is always available to you except when you choose not to hear it. Ego will make you think you are not loved, not worthy and are alone. When this happens, close your eyes, feel your non-physical self, right by your side, telling you to stop indulging in the negative and feel the love and encouragement that is so vastly yours.

You are in a human body on a spiritual journey and nothing in this existence can harm you unless you let it. You let it by believing you are weak and incapable. Visualize the beautiful light that surrounds you and protects you always and don't let the negative or EGO prevail.

*You don't have to TRY to make bad thoughts go away, just have different thoughts. You can refer back in the book where A Student of Satori gave some personal examples of her own negative thoughts reflecting on how they made her feel as opposed to just changing the words expressing a more grateful attitude and thought process then experiencing the difference in the FEELING positive talk brought.

*Remember we all have a story, OUR story.

Your story is your story and no one else's. We all experience in different ways, process in different ways, need different things for our OWN reasons. As we grow up and move out into the world on our own we forget OUR story and tend to carry with us what has been dictated to us as children carrying forward our misguided understandings.

In the quest to live our authentic lives, find our power and love ourselves we must remember and practice allowing, forgiving and perspective. Just because you feel or see something one way does not mean it is right for someone else or that you should be the one to decide that.

Life is hard and we can always count on it to bring constant challenges to our door with a spin of confusion and frustration.

*It is our job to keep in perspective what is real and matters, that being our eternal selves. Keeping your eye on what is will only bring more of the same. Change your focus and your mindset, never stop asking "What do I want" or telling yourself you deserve it.

*Never stop purposely learning or practicing allowing. For me this seems to be the key in a successful lesson learned.

Our goal must be to learn lessons successfully and move on. We have to be committed to continuous purposeful acts of change and that requires self-examination into our daily lives acknowledging how we deal with situations and people including how we react ultimately deciding on a direction to take.

Thank you for reading my book and opening your heart to the consideration that there is more to us than this physical body and that we are all powerful beings constantly learning how to tap into our power and divine right to be happy.

Be happy my friends love always and believe in YOU.

A Student of Satori

Printed in the United States
by Baker & Taylor Publisher Services